THE ETERNAL GIFT OF GOD

Joy

HAMP LEE III

(com)mission™
PUBLISHING

MONTGOMERY, ALABAMA

Joy: The Eternal Gift of God / Hamp Lee III. 1st ed.

Library of Congress Control Number: 2017907318
ISBN: 978-1-940042-55-8

Contents

Thou wilt shew me the path of life: in thy presence is fulness of joy; at thy right hand there are pleasures for evermore.

PSALM 16:11

Introduction

Webster's Dictionary defines joy as an emotion brought on by well-being, success, or a good future. It is a state of happiness or bliss; a source or cause of delight. The Bible further identifies joy through a wide range of experiences and emotions, such as gladness, calm delight, and rejoicing.

In a world that often demands more than it gives, experiencing joy can seem elusive. Relationships end. Your loved ones become sick or injured. Money problems. Car troubles. Work issues. Sometimes you just want one thing to go your way for once. You want your moment to dance and shout. You want joy.

You know having joy is not some fantasy or myth because you see others experiencing it. They tell their testimonies of God's goodness, grace, and peace, and you cannot help but want it too. You do not want to be envious of what they have. You only want a little slice of joy for yourself.

The thief cometh not, but for to steal, and to kill, and to destroy: I am come that they might have life, and that they might have it more abundantly.

JOHN 10:10

Jesus came to the earth so that you can have an abundant life. He came so that you might experience joy—a joy no one can take from you.

I wrote *Joy: The Eternal Gift of God* as a short dialogue on how you can experience the fullness of joy. This book will address several obstacles to having joy and how you can find and keep your joy as you await the reward of eternal life.

Joy in Nouns

One of the first lessons I remember in school was learning about nouns. A noun is a person, place, or thing. It is something physical I can touch, taste, or see.

Along with my school lessons, the world taught me that to be happy and joyous, I needed an abundance of nouns in my life. I was taught that nouns could boost my self-esteem, self-worth, and social status. So I went after nouns with everything I had.

But no matter how many people I had in my life, places I traveled, or possessions I accumulated, it was never enough. Satisfaction and joy were always temporary. Money could not do it. People could not provide it. Vacations could not change it. And even though I knew I could not find happiness or joy in these things, I kept chasing after them. To be honest, that was all I knew. I did not know any other way to live. Then one day I met Jesus.

I heard people talk about God before. I even attended a few services with my grandmother growing up. But never like this. After a couple Sundays of listening to a preacher while away on business in Alaska, I wanted to become a Christian. When I spoke to my wife about it, she thought it was some ploy to get her to think differently about me.

At the time, we had been married for a few months. Before I left, we were having a lot of marital problems. But when I heard about Jesus, I believed He could fix my marriage.

I was not thinking about who Jesus was, how He died on the cross for my sins, or even what He expected from me as His child. I only saw how He could make my life better and give me the joy I have always wanted—a happy wife and a happy life...*with eternal life*.

Many of us expected our belief in God would make our lives better. We confess our love and belief in Jesus, attend weekly church services, volunteer at the church, and even give to others from time to time. *So why would I have to endure anything painful or tragic? Why would love fail and people turn on me? Why would I feel alone when I am surrounded by people? Why would I lose the things I worked so hard to get?*

One day, a man ran to Jesus. He kneeled before Him and asked what he could do to inherit eternal life.[1] Jesus reminded the man of the commandments.

---

[1] Mark 10:17–31.

He said do not commit adultery, do not kill, do not steal, do not bear false witness, do not defraud anyone, and honor your father and mother. The man told Jesus he had done all these things from his youth.

Jesus said there was one thing he lacked. He needed to sell everything he owned and give it to the poor to have treasure in heaven. Then, he should come, take up his cross, and follow Him. The man became sad when he heard Jesus' response because he owned many possessions. He went away grieved.

After speaking to the rich man, Jesus told His disciples how hard it is for rich people to enter the kingdom of God. He said it was easier for a camel to go through the eye of a needle than for a rich man to enter the kingdom of God.

The disciples were astonished. They were saying among themselves, *"Who then can be saved?"* Even though they left everything they had, they questioned their own 'place' in the kingdom of God.[2]

See, the rich man understood that to enter the kingdom of God, it was all or nothing. Jesus made it very plain to him. And though he had a form of godliness and was religiously pious, God was not his true lord or source of joy. His possessions were.[3]

Even though such conditions for entering the kingdom of God remain today, many of us do not

---

[2] Mark 10:28.

[3] 2 Timothy 3:5.

come to the same conclusion as the rich man. We do not translate a life in Christ as all or nothing. Because of our desire to live a better life on earth, we want God and possessions...or at least God's help to obtain them.[4]

We expect nothing but God's best—in every moment of everyday—even though we offer far less in return. And as long as life is going well, we are happy. But the moment tragedy or something negative occurs, we become angry, question God, and want to turn away from Him grieved.

Jesus wanted His disciples to understand that all things are possible for God. You can enter the kingdom of God. Jesus told them that those who left their house, brothers, sisters, father, mother, wife, children, or lands—for His and the gospel's sake—would receive a hundred times more in this life houses, brothers and sisters, mothers and children, and lands *with persecutions*. And in the world to come, they would receive eternal life.[5]

The key words in Jesus' statement are '*for His and the gospel's sake.*' Such individuals who give up all do so for Jesus and the gospel. God becomes their true source of joy, not people, places, or things. When Jesus adds houses, brothers and sisters, mothers and children, and lands *with persecutions*, their trust

---

[4] Matthew 6:24.

[5] Mark 10:29–30.

remains in God. Their joy is fixed upon Him, not on the things He provides.

True joy is found in God alone: to know Him, love Him, and be in His presence for all eternity.[6] God is the steady compass who never changes.[7] And as long as your compass is set on nouns, you will never find your way home. You will remain in the wilderness of life seeking people, places, and things that waste away and fade instead of seeking a place that will last forever.

---

[6] Psalm 16:11.

[7] Malachi 3:6; James 1:17.

Joy of Heaven

Jesus appointed seventy people to go out ahead of Him.[8] He said, "*The harvest truly is great, but the labourers are few: pray ye therefore the Lord of the harvest, that he would send forth labourers into his harvest.*"[9] Jesus was sending them in pairs of two as lambs among wolves.[10] He had provided specific instructions for the seventy before they went out.[11]

When the seventy returned, they came to Jesus with joy. They were excited about what they accomplished. The seventy said, "*Lord, even the devils*

---

[8] Luke 10:1.

[9] Luke 10:2.

[10] Luke 10:3.

[11] Luke 10:3–11.

are subject unto us through thy name."[12] Jesus told them that He saw Satan fall from heaven like lightning. He also said He was giving them the authority to tread on serpents and scorpions, and over all the power of the enemy. Nothing would hurt them in any way.[13]

Today, God sends many laborers into His harvest. Like the seventy, some rejoice over the power and people they were given from God. As the harvest (of souls) is truly great, there are five things each laborer must understand:

1. The work is great and cannot be accomplished by one person. You should pray that God will send people into His harvest around the world, in places you can and cannot personally reach.

2. You are not alone in laboring for God. Do not hinder other believers in Christ who do not serve the Lord as you do or serve in like fellowships, ministries, and churches.[14]

3. Do not show favoritism among fellow workers.[15] Where there is jealousy, strife, and divisions among believers over the importance, allegiance, or

---

[12] Luke 10:17.

[13] Luke 10:18–19.

[14] Mark 9:33–50.

[15] Matthew 18:1–4, 20:25–28; Acts 10:34–35; Romans 2:1–13; James 2:1–9.

preference of one specific laborer over another, Paul considers such behavior as carnal and fleshly.[16]

Each laborer is only a servant whom others come to believe, as the Lord provides them.[17] One person plants and another person waters, but God gives the increase.[18] Laborers serve together with God as His fellow workers.[19]

4. It is the Lord's harvest, not yours. No laborer or person from among His harvest belongs to you.[20] You are a laborer given the privilege to serve and minister to a particular person or group for a specific amount of time. The number of people you are privileged to serve and minister to—whether one or one million— is of no specific importance. Each laborer is given a measure of faith and work based on his or her ability.[21] Be faithful where God sends you and with what He calls you to do.[22]

5. Do not lord over God's harvest. Two of Jesus' disciples, James and John, and their mother came to

---

[16] 1 Corinthians 3:3–4.

[17] 1 Corinthians 3:5.

[18] 1 Corinthians 3:6–8.

[19] 1 Corinthians 3:9.

[20] Jesus purchased us through the blood He shed (1 Corinthians 6:20, 7:23).

[21] Matthew 25:14–30; Romans 12:3–8.

[22] Matthew 9:35–38.

Him. She kneeled before Him and asked that He command her sons to sit on His right and left hand in His Kingdom—positions of honor and authority.[23]

Jesus said they did not know what they were asking for. He asked James and John if they were able to drink the cup He was about to drink, and be baptized with the baptism He is baptized with.[24] When James and John said they were able, Jesus said they would indeed drink His cup and be baptized with the same baptism. But He told them the positions on His right and left hand were not His to assign. His Father has prepared those positions for the ones He has chosen.[25]

When the ten disciples overheard their discussion, they became angry with James and John. Jesus called them together and said the rulers of the nations and the great ones exercise authority over them.[26] But they shall not conduct themselves like this. He said *whoever* will be great among them, let him be your minister, and *whoever* will be chief (and first) among them, let him be your servant—just as He did not

---

[23] Matthew 20:20–21.

[24] Matthew 20:22.

[25] Matthew 20:23.

[26] Matthew 20:24–25.

come to be ministered to, but to minister to others, and give His life as a ransom for many.[27]

Jesus said a disciple is not above his teacher nor a servant above his master. He said it is enough for disciples to be like their teacher and servants like their master.[28]

As Jesus described to His disciples, you should not seek to exercise authority over those the Father has given you. If you want to be great and first among those in your fellowship, you must be their minister and servant.

Nevertheless, don't rejoice in this, that the spirits are subject to you, but rejoice that your names are written in heaven.

LUKE 10:20

Jesus told the seventy not to rejoice that the spirits are subject to them, but to rejoice that their names are written in heaven. He said this to emphasize where they should place their affections. Their joy must be set on the things above and not on things of the world.[29] The world and every one of its desires—lust of the eyes and flesh and the pride of life—will pass

---

[27] Matthew 20:26–28.

[28] Matthew 10:24–25.

[29] Colossians 3:2.

away. But their future inheritance is incorruptible, undefiled, and does not fade way.[30]

The opportunity to experience the joy of heaven has been shared with the world. Nothing in the world can compare with the riches of heaven—not power, possession, or position. These will all expire and pass away, but the joy of heaven is forever. Set your affections on heaven and the joy to come. Rejoice that your name is written in heaven. *Rejoice!*

---

[30] 2 Corinthians 4:17–18; Hebrews 11:1; 1 Peter 1:3–9.

Joy & Strength

Then he said unto them, Go your way, eat the fat, and drink the sweet, and send portions unto them for whom nothing is prepared: for this day is holy unto our Lord: neither be ye sorry; for the joy of the Lord is your strength.

NEHEMIAH 8:10

When the returned exiles gathered together in the streets, Ezra, the scribe and priest, read the book of the law of Moses from morning until midday. The Levites and several others helped the people understand the reading. As the people were weeping over what they heard, Nehemiah, the governor, spoke to them. He told them that this day was holy unto the Lord their God and not to mourn or weep. Nehemiah told them to go their way, eat the fat, drink the sweet, and provide for those who had nothing prepared, for the day was holy unto the Lord. They should not be grieved because the joy of the Lord was their strength. After the Levites had quieted the people, they went their way to eat, drink, send portions to those without, and to celebrate.

Why is the Lord's joy your strength?

God delights in His creation.

The Lord thy God in the midst of thee is mighty; he will save, he will rejoice over thee with joy; he will rest in his love, he will joy over thee with singing.

ZEPHANIAH 3:17

Of all that God created, man is the only creation made in His image.[31] He created us for Himself, for His glory.[32] God created man to enjoy an eternal fellowship with Him. He blessed man and woman and gave them dominion over every living thing that moved upon the earth.[33]

Though Satan sought to disrupt this eternal fellowship by tempting Eve in the garden of Eden, we witness God's redemptive work for His creation.[34] In spite of Adam's disobedience and sin, He provided

[31] Genesis 1:27, 5:1–2.

[32] Isaiah 43:5–7, 21.

[33] Genesis 1:26–28.

[34] Genesis 3.

for them and foretold a prophecy concerning Jesus.[35] When what He foretold would come to pass, God would re-establish the eternal fellowship between Himself and His creation.[36]

Throughout the biblical record, we witness the unfolding of God's story between Himself and His creation. Even in times when His chosen people disobeyed and acted against His commands, God would not utterly forsake or consume them. When the people turned back to Him, He would protect them and provide deliverance from their oppressors.[37]

God is love.

Beloved, let us love one another: for love is of God; and every one that loveth is born of God, and knoweth God. He that loveth not knoweth not God; for God is love. In this was manifested the love of God toward us, because that God sent his only begotten Son into the world, that we might live through him. Herein is love, not that we loved God, but that he loved us, and sent his Son to be the propitiation for our sins.

1 JOHN 4:7–10

---

[35] Genesis 3:15.

[36] Isaiah 9:6–7; Matthew 1:23; Luke 1:31–33; Romans 16:20; Galatians 4:4–5.

[37] Nehemiah 9:26–31.

God is love. He is the very definition and essence of love. Love is defined as affection or kindness, a feast of charity. The Bible describes charity in several ways:[38]

1. suffers long (patiently endures),
2. is kind,
3. does not envy,
4. does not boast,
5. is not prideful,
6. does not behave unseemly,
7. is not selfish,
8. is not easily provoked,
9. thinks no evil,
10. does not rejoice over sin,
11. rejoices in the truth,
12. never fails.

In His love, God sent His only begotten Son into the world to give His life for the sins of mankind.[39] God sacrificed Himself for His creation.[40] He died to re-establish the eternal fellowship between you and His Father.

---

[38] 1 Corinthians 13:4–8.

[39] John 3:16–17.

[40] John 1:1–4, 14.

God delights in you.

Out of the billions of people on the planet, God chose you. He wants you to experience the greatest joy imaginable: eternal life in His presence.

God's joy is your strength because of the lengths He has taken to bring His creation back to Himself. Consider what He has done to reveal His love to you over your life. God has protected you, covered you, and blessed you. He has been with you through the highest highs and the lowest lows. And regardless of where you have been—positionally or physically—He wants you to experience His love and grace firsthand.

God delights in sharing His joy.

It is not God's will for even one person to be lost.[41] He takes no pleasure in the destruction of the wicked.[42] God desires to share His love with His creation. And as you come to Him and experience His love, He sends you to places near and far to display His love, testify of His goodness, and bring glory to His name.[43] The same love He extended to you, He wants to share with the world.

God wants you to be a part of the greatest love story ever written. He delights in you and wants to

---

[41] 2 Peter 3:9.

[42] Ezekiel 18:23, 33:11; 1 Timothy 2:1–4.

[43] Isaiah 43:5–7; Matthew 5:14–16; John 13:34–35.

spend an eternity with you and so many others. He wants you to experience the fullness of joy.[44]

---

[44] Psalm 16:11.

Experiencing Joy

O taste and see that the Lord is good: blessed is the
man that trusteth in him.

PSALMS 34:8

To experience joy is to experience God. An experience in God is far more than receiving His protection or provision. Experiencing God comes through uniquely personal encounters through His word, praise and worship, prayer, and your fellowship with other believers. These encounters draw you closer to God; directing your heart into His love and teaching you how to place your complete trust in Him.[45]

---

[45] Psalm 73:28; 2 Thessalonians 3:5.

Bible

Through the pages of the Bible, God describes His story of love and redemption. As I read more of God's word, I learned that His story is also my story. I am a part of His family, and as His child, God describes the life He desires to have with me today and in the future.[46]

The Bible is also my manual for daily living. His word is living and active, discerning the thoughts and intents of my heart.[47] By instructing, correcting, rebuking, protecting, and training me in righteousness, God's word is teaching me how to live as His child.[48]

Blessed is the man that walketh not in the counsel of the ungodly, nor standeth in the way of sinners, nor sitteth in the seat of the scornful. But his delight is in the law of the Lord; and in his law doth he meditate day and night. And he shall be like a tree planted by the rivers of water, that bringeth forth his fruit in his

---

[46] John 1:9–13; Romans 8:12–17, 11:11–24; Galatians 3:23–29; Ephesians 1:11–14; 1 Peter 1:1–12; 1 John 3:1–3.

[47] Hebrews 4:12.

[48] Psalm 119:103; Proverbs 30:5; Matthew 5–7, 28:18–20; Luke 6:40; John 3:19–21, 8:31–32, 13:34–35; Romans 8:28–29, 12:1–2; 2 Corinthians 5:17–21; Ephesians 4:17–32; 1 Timothy 4:8; 2 Timothy 3:16–17; 1 John 2:1–6

season; his leaf also shall not wither; and whatsoever he doeth shall prosper.

PSALM 1:1-3

Prayer

When I read about the beautiful and intimate relationship David shared with the Lord through the Psalms, it allowed me to see how a man can commune with God. There were no situations, conversations, or topics that were off-limits. I saw how I could bare my soul and pour out my heart before Him.[49]

As I bared my soul and poured out my heart, God filled me with His grace, love, and peace. He was my refuge and very present help in trouble.[50] When I lifted my eyes to the hills, God helped me to lift my heart, soul, and mind above my circumstances; to see life from His perspective rather than my own.[51] He led me toward green pastures of peace and still waters for my soul.[52]

---

[49] Psalm 62:8, Isaiah 1:18; Philippians 4:6; Hebrews 4:14–16; James 1:5–8; 1 John 5:14–15.

[50] Psalm 46:1-3.

[51] Psalm 121:1–2; Proverbs 12:5; 2 Corinthians 5:16–17; Titus 1:15; 1 Peter 1:13–16.

[52] Psalm 23.

God speaks to me through His Spirit to lead and guide me; to remind me of His promises and will.[53] He encourages me to persevere and walk in the Spirit.[54]

Praise and Worship

Praise is a celebration toward God.[55] It is an expression of singing, shouting, dance, and music.[56] Worship is an homage to God; to bow down, fall down flat, humbly seek, reverence, stoop, or show deep respect.[57] Together, praise and worship are intentional, outward expressions to celebrate and show adoration and reverence to God.

Praise and worship are experiences that saturate and engulf your heart, soul, and mind in the Lord. In the purest moments I experienced before the Father, I saw my praise and worship as gifts unto Him; to acknowledge His sovereignty in my life and to honor Him.

---

[53] John 14:26, 16:13.

[54] Psalm 28, 138:3; Proverbs 24:16; Mark 13:1–13; Romans 5:3–5; Galatians 6:9–10; Philippians 3:13–14; Hebrews 3:1–6, 10:36–39; James 1:2–4, 5:10–11; 2 Peter 1:4–11.

[55] Psalm 34:1–3, 63:3–4, 66:1–3, 95:1–3, 100, Ephesians 5:19–21; Hebrews 13:15–16.

[56] Psalm 21:13, 33:1–3, 89:1, 96:2–4, 103:2–5, 113:1–4, 134, 145:1–3, 150; Colossians 3:16.

[57] Psalm 29:2, 95:6; John 4:23–24; Romans 12:1–2; Philippians 3:3.

Praise and worship are experiences that extend far beyond the walls of the church. Through every moment and experience I have throughout the day, I should give thanks to God.[58] I should worship God in the shower, while traveling, and through my daily interactions with others. I show honor and reverence to God by placing Him first—above all other people, places, and things.[59]

Fellowship

The fellowship of the saints can be a great encouragement for remaining joyous and focused on the Lord. Such fellowships are of like-minded and loving people who are honest, caring, supportive, and encouraging.[60] These relationships are founded and result in personal or corporate edification and growth in holiness and obedience to the Lord.[61]

Iron sharpeneth iron; so a man sharpeneth the countenance of his friend.

PROVERBS 27:17

---

[58] 1 Thessalonians 5:18.

[59] Matthew 6:24–34; Hebrews 13:15–16.

[60] Proverbs 12:20, 15:23, 17:17, 18:24, 27:9, 17; Ecclesiastes 4:8–12; Philippians 2:1–4.

[61] Proverbs 27:6; John 17:20–21; Romans 14:19; Hebrews 10:24–25.

These experiences over the past twenty years are my personal testimonies of my experiences in God. They are a part of His work to plant me as a tree of righteousness, to taste and see how truly good He is, and to glorify Him through my life.[62]

As your personal story is being shaped before the Lord, you might experience great success or great tragedy. You might even have more questions than answers. And though you cannot explain why certain events and situations are allowed to happen, it is important to know that God's love for you is undeniable.[63] Even in the lowest of days, God will not leave you.[64] He will guide and comfort you.[65] God will strengthen you when you are weak and cover you with His grace.[66] He is faithful in the good. He is faithful in the bad. God is your steady rock and the lighthouse in the midst of your storms—your source of peace at every turn.

God often uses trying and difficult situations to expand your perspective, deepen your love and trust in Him, and perfect you.[67] God will not give you

---

[62] Psalm 34:8; Isaiah 61:1–3; Matthew 5:14–16.

[63] Psalm 63:3, 108:4; Isaiah 55:8–9; Ephesians 2:4–7; 1 John 4:19.

[64] Hebrews 13:5.

[65] Psalm 25:4–5, 32:8, 73:23–24, 119:33; Proverbs 3:5–6, 16:9.

[66] 2 Corinthians 12:8–10.

[67] James 1:2–4.

anything you cannot handle.[68]   He desires the excellency of His grace and power to shine through your life:[69]

But we have this treasure in earthen vessels, that the excellency of the power may be of God, and not of us. We are troubled on every side, yet not distressed; we are perplexed, but not in despair; Persecuted, but not forsaken; cast down, but not destroyed; Always bearing about in the body the dying of the Lord Jesus, that the life also of Jesus might be made manifest in our body. For we which live are always delivered unto death for Jesus' sake, that the life also of Jesus might be made manifest in our mortal flesh.

2 CORINTHIANS 4:7–11

God wants you to experience Him in a very personal and intimate way. Your experiences might be different from my own, but they should testify of God so His glory can be seen through your life.[70] He is working in you and through you for your ultimate good.[71] This is so you can receive what no person, place, or thing can take away from you—joy in His presence forever.

---

[68] 1 Corinthians 10:13.

[69] 2 Corinthians 12:7–10.

[70] Matthew 5:14–16.

[71] Philippians 1:6.

Full of Joy

After eating the Passover with His disciples, Jesus knew the time to leave the earth and return to the Father had come.[72] He shared several messages to comfort and instruct them so that their joy might be full.

Receive Jesus' Joy—John 13:31–15:11

1. Jesus referred to the disciples as 'little children.' He said He would only be with them a little while longer. The disciples will seek for Him, but where He is going, they cannot come. Though they cannot follow Jesus now, they will follow Him afterward.[73]

2. Jesus provided a new commandment: to love one another. As Jesus loved the disciples, they should also love one another.[74] This is how everyone will know they are His disciples.

---

[72] John 13:1.

[73] John 13:33.

[74] John 13:34–35.

3. Peter asked where Jesus was going. When He said Peter could not follow Him now but afterward, Peter wondered why. Peter said he would lay his life down for Him. In response, Jesus said Peter would deny Him three times before the rooster crows.[75]

4. Jesus told the disciples not to let their hearts be troubled; to believe in God and in Him.[76]

5. Jesus said He was going to prepare a place in His Father's house for them, as there are many homes there.[77]

6. If Jesus were going to prepare a place for them, He would come again to receive them to Himself, and bring them to His Father's house.[78]

7. Jesus said they will know the way to the Father's house. Thomas asked, *"Lord, we know not whither thou goest; and how can we know the way?"* Jesus said He is the way, the truth, and the life. No one comes to the Father except through Him.[79]

8. Jesus said if the disciples had known Him, they would have known His Father also. And from now on, they know the Father and have seen Him. Jesus is in the Father, and the Father is in Him. Jesus and the

---

[75] John 13:36–38.

[76] John 14:1.

[77] John 14:2.

[78] John 14:3.

[79] John 14:4–6.

Father are one.[80] The Father, who lives in Jesus, does His works through Jesus. This is the proof that He is in the Father and the Father is in Him.[81]

9. Because Jesus is going back to His Father, those who believe in Him will do the same works and even greater works.[82]

10. Jesus will do whatever the disciples ask in His name so that the Father might be glorified in the Son.[83]

11. If the disciples love Jesus, they should keep His commandments. When they do, Jesus will pray to the Father to give them another Comforter. He will be with them forever.[84]

12. The Comforter, also identified as the Spirit of truth, cannot be received by the world because they neither see Him nor know Him. However, the disciples will know Him because He will live with them and be in them.[85]

13. Jesus told the disciples He will not leave them comfortless but will come to them.[86]

---

[80] John 14:7–11; 1 John 5:7.

[81] John 14:7–11.

[82] John 14:12.

[83] John 14:13–14.

[84] John 14:15–16.

[85] John 14:17.

[86] John 14:18.

14. In a little while, the world will no longer see Jesus due to His crucifixion. But the disciples will see Him again. Because He will rise from the dead and live, the disciples will live in eternity with Him.[87] In that day, the disciples will know that Jesus is in His Father, they are in Him, and Jesus is in them.[88]

15. People who love Jesus will have and keep His commandments. The Father will love those who love Jesus and Jesus will love them and reveal Himself to them.[89]

16. Judas (not Iscariot) asked what has happened that Jesus is about to reveal Himself to the disciples and not the world. Jesus answered by saying if a man loves Him, he will keep Jesus' word. The Father will love the man, and both He and the Father will come to him and make their home with him. But Jesus said those who do not love Him do not keep His words, for His words are from the Father who sent Him.[90]

17. When the Father sends the Comforter—which is Holy Spirit—in Jesus' name, He will teach them all things and remind them of everything Jesus said to them.[91]

---

[87] Romans 6:1–10.

[88] John 14:19–20.

[89] John 14:21.

[90] John 14:22–25.

[91] John 14:26.

18. Jesus is leaving them His peace, but not as the world gives.[92] He told them not to let their hearts be troubled or fearful. He is going away and coming to them. If they loved Him, they would have rejoiced in hearing that He was going to His Father, as the Father is greater than Him.[93]

19. Jesus told them all these things before they happen so that when they do occur, they might believe. Jesus told them He would not speak much more to them because the prince of the world (Satan) was coming, but he has nothing in Him. This was so that the world might know that Jesus loves the Father and has done what the Father commanded Him to do.[94]

20. As Jesus and His disciples departed from their location, He talked about remaining in Him.[95] He said He is the true vine, and His Father is the farmer. The Father takes away every branch in Jesus that does not bear fruit.[96] But for every branch that does bear fruit, He prunes so that they can bear more fruit.

---

[92] Romans 11:29.

[93] John 14:27–28.

[94] John 14:29–31.

[95] John 14:31.

[96] Matthew 3:1–10, 7:17–20; John 15:1–2.

Jesus said the disciples were already pruned clean because of the word He spoke to them.[97]

21. Jesus told the disciples to remain in Him, and He will remain in them. Branches cannot bear fruit by themselves. They must remain connected to the vine. He reminds them that He is the vine and they are the branches. They can bear fruit as long as they remain in Him (and He in them)—for apart from Jesus—they can do nothing.[98]

22. If someone does not remain in Him, they will be thrown out as a branch and wither. The angels will gather them at the end of the age and throw them into the fire to be burned.[99]

23. If the disciples remain in Jesus and His word remains in them, they can ask whatever they desire, and it will be done for them. Jesus will do whatever the disciples ask in His name so that the Father might be glorified in the Son.[100] When the disciples bear a lot of fruit, the Father will be glorified, and they will prove to be His disciples.[101]

24. Jesus has loved the disciples as the Father has loved Him. He told them to remain in His love by

---

[97] John 15:3.

[98] John 15:4–5.

[99] Matthew 24:31, 25:31–33, 41–46; John 15:6–7.

[100] John 14:13–14, 15:7.

[101] John 15:8.

keeping His commandments, as He has kept His Father's commandments and remained in His love. Jesus spoke these things so that His joy would remain in them and that their joy would be made full.[102] Their joy will be made full as they complete the work He called them to accomplish on earth (as Jesus had) and enter the kingdom of God.

Full of Joy—John 15:12–16:24

1. Jesus gave the disciples His commandment: to love one another as He loved them. He said no one has a greater love for a friend than laying down their life for them. Whoever does what Jesus commands is His friend.[103]

2. Jesus no longer called the disciples servants because servants do not know what their master is doing. They were now friends because everything Jesus heard from the Father, He made known to them.[104]

3. Jesus chose the disciples to go and bear fruit. They did not choose Him. He did this so that their fruit might remain. And whatever they ask the Father in Jesus' name will be given to them. Jesus

---

[102] John 15:9–11. Jesus' joy was redeeming His creation (Hebrews 12:1-2). Here, the joy He speaks of is the joy of eternal life, sharing an eternity with them in the Father's presence (Psalm 16:11).

[103] John 15:12–14.

[104] John 15:15.

commanded these things so they might love one another.[105]

4. If the world hates the disciples, they should know it hated Jesus first. The world would love them if they were of it, but because they are not, the world will hate them because Jesus chose them out of the world.[106]

5. Jesus reminds them of what He said about a servant not being greater than his lord. If the world persecuted Him, they would also be persecuted. But if they had kept Jesus' word, they would keep theirs as well.[107]

6. The world will hate and persecute the disciples on account of Jesus because they do not know the Father. If Jesus had not come and spoken to them, they would not have sinned, but because He came and spoke to them, they have no excuse for their sin. They have seen and hated both Jesus and the Father. But this happened so that the word might be fulfilled, '*They hated me without a cause.*'[108]

7. Jesus said when He sends the Comforter to them from the Father, the Comforter will testify about Him. The disciples will also testify about Him

---

[105] John 15:16–17.

[106] John 15:18–19.

[107] John 15:20.

[108] Psalms 35:19, 69:4, 109:3; John 15:21–25.

because they have been with Him from the beginning.[109]

8. Jesus told the disciples these things so that they would not have any cause to stumble. They will be put out of the synagogues. The time will come when whoever kills them will believe they are offering a service to God. They will do these things because they do not know the Father or Jesus. But Jesus was telling them these things now so that when these times do come, they will remember what He said. He did not tell them these things from the beginning because He was with them. Now, Jesus is going to the Father, but none of the disciples asked, *"Where are you going?"*[110]

9. Jesus said because He told the disciples these things, sorrow filled their hearts. But He reminded them that it is to their advantage for Him to leave. If Jesus leaves, He will send the Comforter to them.[111]

10. When the Comforter comes, He will convict the world of three things: sin, righteousness, and judgment. He will convict the world of sin because they do not believe in Him. He will convict the world of righteousness because Jesus is going to His Father and they will not see Him any longer. He will convict

---

[109] John 15:26–27.

[110] John 16:1–5.

[111] John 16:6–7.

the world of judgment because the prince of this world is judged.[112]

11. Though Jesus had many things to tell the disciples, He said they could not bear them now. But when the Spirit of truth comes, He will guide them into all truth. He will only speak what He hears. The Spirit of truth will not speak of Himself. He will declare things that are to come. The Spirit of truth will glorify Jesus and take what is His and declare it to the disciples. Jesus said everything the Father has is His. This is why He said the Spirit of truth will take what is His and declare it to them.[113]

12. Jesus told the disciples that in a little while they would not see Him, but in a little while, they would. When Jesus perceived the disciples wanted to ask Him what He meant by this statement, He said they will weep and lament while the world rejoices. The disciples will be sorrowful, but one day their sorrow will be turned to joy. He gave the illustration of a woman giving birth. Jesus said while she gives birth, she has sorrow because the time of birth has come. But when she delivers the child, she no longer remembers her anguish. She is joyful because her child is born into the world. Likewise, the disciples will have sorrow, but they will see Him again. Their hearts will rejoice, and no one will be able to take their joy

---

[112] John 16:8–11.

[113] John 16:12–15.

from them, for in that day, the disciples will ask no questions.[114]

13. Jesus reiterates that whatever they ask of the Father in His name, the Father will give it to them. Up to this point, the disciples had not asked for anything in His name. If they ask, they will receive, so that their joy might be full.[115]

Receiving whatever they ask in Jesus' name is help in being faithful until the end, maintaining a strong testimony and witness, and furthering the gospel. Their asking has everything to do with loving God, bringing glory to the Father, and finishing the work He gave them to do.

Joy Fulfilled in Themselves—John 16:24–17:13

1. Jesus spoke these things to the disciples in proverbs (figures of speech). But He said the time will come when He will speak plainly about the Father. In that day, the disciples will ask the Father in Jesus' name. Jesus will not say to them that He will pray to the Father on their behalf, for the Father Himself loves them because they loved Jesus and believed He came from God.[116]

---

[114] John 16:16–22; Revelation 21:1–4.

[115] John 16:23–24.

[116] John 16:25–27.

2. Jesus said He came from the Father and has come into the world. Now, He will leave the world and go back to the Father.[117]

3. The disciples mentioned how Jesus now speaks plainly to them. They said they now know He knows all things and does not need anyone to question Him. By this, they believe Jesus came from God.[118]

4. Jesus responded by saying, *"Do you now believe?"* He told them the time is coming (and has come) when they will all be scattered. Each of them will go to their own place and leave Him alone. But Jesus said He was not alone because the Father will be with Him. Jesus told them these things because—in Him—the disciples will have peace, though they will face tribulation and oppression in the world.[119] But Jesus tells them to be of good cheer (have comfort and courage) because He has overcome the world.[120]

5. Jesus lifted His eyes up to heaven to pray. He said the time has come. He asked the Father to glorify

---

[117] John 16:28.

[118] John 16:29–30.

[119] John 16:31–33.

[120] Jesus has overcome the world, gaining the victory over death and hades (1 Corinthians 15:55–58; Revelation 1:18). Everyone who believes that Jesus is the Christ is born of God and overcomes the world (1 John 4:4, 5:3–5).

the Son so that the Son might also glorify the Father.[121]

6. As the Father gave Jesus authority over all mankind, He will give eternal life to everyone the Father gives Him.[122]

7. Jesus said eternal life is that they should know the Father, the only true God and Jesus, whom He sent.[123]

8. Jesus said He glorified the Father on earth. He accomplished the work the Father gave Him to do. Jesus asked the Father to glorify Him—with His own self—with the glory He had with the Father before the world existed.[124]

9. Jesus revealed the Father's name to the people the Father gave Him.[125]

10. Jesus said they now know that all things He received from the Father are from Him because He gave them all the words He received. They received them and know, for sure, that Jesus came from the Father and believe the Father sent Him.[126]

---

[121] John 17:1.

[122] John 17:2.

[123] John 17:3.

[124] John 17:4–5.

[125] John 17:6. The name He was given was Jesus (John 17:11; Hebrews 1:4).

[126] John 17:7–8.

11. Jesus said He prays for those the Father gives Him and not the world because they are the Father's. He says all things that are His are the Father's and all things that are the Father's are His. Jesus is glorified in them.[127]

12. Jesus said He will no longer be in the world and will be returning to the Father. But the ones whom the Father gives Him will be in the world. Jesus asked the Father to keep them through the name He gave Him, so they might be one, even as He and the Father are one.[128]

13. While Jesus was with them in the world, He kept them in His Name. He kept those He was given. No one was lost except Judas—the son of perdition—so that the Scripture might be fulfilled.[129]

14. Jesus said He now goes to the Father and what He said in the world was to ensure that they might have His joy fulfilled in themselves.[130]

---

[127] John 17:9–10; Romans 8:14–17.

[128] John 17:11.

[129] Psalm 41:9; John 13:18, 17:12.

[130] John 17:13.

Conclusion of Jesus' Prayer—John 17:14–26

1. Jesus told the Father that He gave the disciples His word. The world hated them because they are not of the world, even as He is not of the world.[131]

2. Jesus prayed that the Father would not take them out of the world. Jesus asked that He would keep them from the evil one. Like Jesus, they are not of the world.[132]

3. Jesus asked that the Father sanctify them in His truth, as His word is truth. As the Father sent Jesus into the world, Jesus sends the disciples into the world. For their sakes, He consecrated Himself so they might be consecrated in truth.[133]

4. Jesus was not only praying for the disciples but for everyone who will believe in Him through the word they share. This is so that we all might be one, even as the Father is in Jesus and Jesus is in the Father. We might be one with them so that the world will believe that the Father sent Jesus.[134]

5. Jesus gave the glory the Father gave Him to the disciples. This is so that they might be one, even as He and the Father are one. Jesus is in them and the Father is in Jesus—that they might be made perfect in one—

---

[131] John 17:14.

[132] John 17:15–16.

[133] John 17:17–19.

[134] John 17:20–21.

so that the world might know the Father sent Jesus and the Father loved them, even as the Father loved Jesus.[135]

6. Jesus desired that those whom the Father gave Him will be with Him where He is and will see His glory—which the Father gave Him—as He loved Jesus before the foundation of the world.[136]

7. Jesus called the Father righteous and said the world has not known Him, but He did, and the disciples knew that the Father sent Him. Jesus made the Father's name known to them and will make it known to others so that the love the Father loved Jesus with will be in them and Jesus will be in them.[137]

---

[135] John 17:22–23.

[136] John 17:24.

[137] John 17:25–26.

Enduring Joy

Wherefore seeing we also are compassed about with so great a cloud of witnesses, let us lay aside every weight, and the sin which doth so easily beset us, and let us run with patience the race that is set before us, Looking unto Jesus the author and finisher of our faith; who for the joy that was set before him endured the cross, despising the shame, and is set down at the right hand of the throne of God. For consider him that endured such contradiction of sinners against himself, lest ye be wearied and faint in your minds. Ye have not yet resisted unto blood, striving against sin.

HEBREWS 12:1–4

The book of Hebrews was written to Hebrew Christians who were facing persecution and were considering a return to Judaism. Its purpose was to present Jesus Christ as perfect and superior in comparison to anything Judaism had to offer.[138] The writer admonished them to persevere and not turn away from their only hope of salvation.

In the first few verses of chapter twelve, the writer describes a cloud of witnesses surrounding them. They were described in the previous chapter for their stance of faith in the face of opposition and persecution. These men and women considered themselves as strangers and pilgrims on the earth, preparing themselves for their true home—a city whose maker and builder is God.[139]

As they did not receive what was promised while living on earth—the promise of eternal life—they stood and died in faith.[140] They embraced the promise from afar and displayed the evidence of their beliefs through their faithful testimonies.[141]

As the Hebrew Christians were surrounded by faithful men and women from their own lineage, the writer provided instructions on how they can persevere and live faithfully unto God. As you are a part of the family of God, you can also be encouraged by these faithful men and women surrounding you:

---

[138] "Hebrews Summary - Bible Hub," Bible Hub, accessed May 15, 2017, http://biblehub.com/summary/hebrews/1.htm.

[139] Hebrews 11:10.

[140] Hebrews 11:13.

[141] Hebrews 11:1–2, 7–40.

Lay aside weights and sins.

Laying aside weights and sins is a personal decision. It is an intentional decision to remove the things you know have entangled you in the past, and have the potential to do so now and in the future.

Laying aside weights and sins is also a continual decision. Satan and your flesh will look for ways to keep these weights and sins in your life.[142] So you must be sober, self-controlled, and watchful.[143] If they come to tempt you, withstand them steadfastly in the faith—keeping in mind the promise of eternal life for those who endure, as well as your brothers and sisters who are also facing similar circumstances.[144]

Run patiently in the race set before you.

When running your race toward the prize of eternal life, you will need patience.[145] To be patient is to endure under difficult circumstances, often persevering in the face of delay without acting in a negative manner. Patience is developed through stressful situations, long quiet seasons, or while under duress, persecution, or temptation.

---

[142] 1 Peter 5:8.

[143] Proverbs 16:32; 2 Timothy 1:7; 1 Peter 4:7.

[144] 1 Peter 5:8–9.

[145] 1 Corinthians 9:24–27.

Temptations test your faith and produce patience within you.[146] They teach you how to live a holy and righteous life so that you might be perfect and complete, lacking nothing. This is why James says you should count it all joy when these temptations come upon you. They are not meant to break you. They are meant to train and build you up in righteousness.

Know ye not that they which run in a race run all, but one receiveth the prize? So run, that ye may obtain. And every man that striveth for the mastery is temperate in all things. Now they do it to obtain a corruptible crown; but we an incorruptible. I therefore so run, not as uncertainly; so fight I, not as one that beateth the air. But I keep under my body, and bring it into subjection: lest that by any means, when I have preached to others, I myself should be a castaway.

1 CORINTHIANS 9:24–27

Looking to Jesus, the author, and finisher of your faith. As you lay aside weights and sins and run with patience, look to Jesus. 'Looking' in this context is defined as consider attentively. This is how you should set your sights upon Jesus as He is the author of your faith in Him.

---

[146] James 1:2–4.

God drew you to Jesus, giving you the faith to believe in Him.[147] But faith in Christ does not end there. Jesus is also the finisher of your faith.

God began a good work in you, and He will see it to completion until the day of Jesus Christ.[148] Jesus will never leave you nor forsake you.[149] He will be with you to shape and guide your life until the day He comes in His glory.[150]

For the joy that was set before Jesus, He endured the cross, despising the shame, and is set down at the right hand of the throne of God. The joy that was set before Jesus was redeeming His creation, offering Himself for the sins of mankind.[151] Through His life and sacrifice, He became the author of eternal salvation, restoring the eternal fellowship between God and His creation.[152] But His sacrifice did not come without a personal cost.

After eating the Passover, Jesus and His disciples went to the Mount of Olives. Leaving the disciples

---

[147] John 6:44; 1 Corinthians 2:9–16.

[148] Philippians 1:6.

[149] Hebrews 13:5.

[150] Matthew 25:31–46. Sanctification is a process of cleansing and preparation. It is a work of the Holy Spirit (in you) to guide, teach, direct, and mold you in holiness (Matthew 5:14–16; John 14:26, 16:13; Romans 8:29).

[151] Romans 5:6–19; Philippians 2:5–11.

[152] Hebrews 5:7–10.

about a stone's throw away, He kneeled down and prayed. He asked the Father, if He was willing, to remove this cup from Him. The cup Jesus was to drink was that of suffering—for the sins of the world placed upon Him.

Jesus was the perfect sacrifice for the sins of the world.[153] There was no other. God had ordained it before the world was created for your glory.[154] This was the will of God.

...nevertheless not my will, but thine, be done.

An angel appeared to Jesus from heaven to strengthen Him. Jesus was in agony, but He prayed even more earnestly. His sweat was like great drops of blood falling to the ground. His sweating can be associated with a condition known as hematidrosis, which occurs under conditions of extreme physical or emotional stress.[155]

Jesus knew exactly what was going to transpire over the next (roughly) fifteen hours. He was going to suffer a very painful and violent death—for you and me.

---

[153] Hebrews 10:1–14.

[154] 1 Corinthians 2:7–9.

[155] Patel, Raksha M., and Stuti Mahajan, "Hematohidrosis: A Rare Clinical Entity," *Indian Dermatology Online Journal* 1.1 (2010): 30–32, accessed May 21, 2017.

...nevertheless not my will, but thine, be done.

During this period, crucifixion was the most shameful and disgraceful form of execution.[156] It was usually reserved for slaves, foreigners, enemies, revolutionaries, and vile criminals.[157] It provided a gruesome and public way to execute criminals and dissenters so that the masses would be dissuaded from breaking the law.[158] But Jesus despised the shame of the cross for the joy that was set before Him:

For he shall grow up before him as a tender plant, and as a root out of a dry ground: he hath no form nor comeliness; and when we shall see him, there is no beauty that we should desire him. He is despised and rejected of men; a man of sorrows, and acquainted with grief: and we hid as it were our faces from him; he was despised, and we esteemed him not. Surely he hath borne our griefs, and carried our sorrows: yet we did esteem him stricken, smitten of God, and afflicted. But he was wounded for our transgressions, he was bruised for our iniquities: the chastisement of our

---

[156] "The Facts of Crucifixion," Catholic Education Resource Center, accessed April 18, 2017,
http://www.catholiceducation.org/en/controversy/common-miscon ceptions/the-facts-of-crucifixion.html.

[157] Ibid.

[158] "Crucifixion," New World Encyclopedia, accessed April 18, 2017, http://www.newworldencyclopedia.org/entry/Crucifixion.

peace was upon him; and with his stripes we are healed. All we like sheep have gone astray; we have turned every one to his own way; and the Lord hath laid on him the iniquity of us all. He was oppressed, and he was afflicted, yet he opened not his mouth: he is brought as a lamb to the slaughter, and as a sheep before her shearers is dumb, so he openeth not his mouth. He was taken from prison and from judgment: and who shall declare his generation? for he was cut off out of the land of the living: for the transgression of my people was he stricken. And he made his grave with the wicked, and with the rich in his death; because he had done no violence, neither was any deceit in his mouth. Yet it pleased the Lord to bruise him; he hath put him to grief: when thou shalt make his soul an offering for sin, he shall see his seed, he shall prolong his days, and the pleasure of the Lord shall prosper in his hand. He shall see of the travail of his soul, and shall be satisfied: by his knowledge shall my righteous servant justify many; for he shall bear their iniquities. Therefore will I divide him a portion with the great, and he shall divide the spoil with the strong; because he hath poured out his soul unto death: and he was numbered with the transgressors; and he bare the sin of many, and made intercession for the transgressors.

ISAIAH 53:2–12

Jesus sacrificed His life for the world.[159] He became the offering for sin God demanded for your iniquity and transgression. By the stripes Jesus willingly accepted in your place, you are healed. His body was broken, and His blood was shed so that you might live.[160]

Consider everything Jesus endured for your redemption. Consider the pain He endured for your reconciliation with God. Consider the peace you experience at the cost of His suffering.

Some will experience significant hardships and others will enjoy seasons of peace. Many might never face circumstances culminating in the shedding of their blood. But no matter where you are in this life, look to Jesus. Remember Him and His example. Allow Jesus' life and sacrifice to encourage you not to become weary, fainthearted, or give up.

Do not allow anyone or anything to disqualify you from the prize of eternal life. Stay before the Father as Jesus had in the Mount of Olives. Read, study, and meditate on His Word, seek Him in prayer and praise and worship, remember His promises, and fellowship with your brothers and sisters in the Lord.

...consider Him.

---

[159] John 3:16.

[160] Matthew 26:26–28; 1 Corinthians 11:23–26.

Testimony of Joy

As joy is an expression of gladness, calm delight, and rejoicing, it also serves as a testimony to the world. One person who had such joy was a man named Stephen. He was described as a man full of faith, the Holy Spirit, and power.[161]

Stephen was doing great wonders and miracles among the people.[162] The Libertines, some of the Cyrenians and Alexandrians, and those from Cilicia and Asia disputed with him. But they were not able to resist the wisdom and spirit by which Stephen spoke.[163] So they induced men to say they heard him speak blasphemous words against Moses and God.

---

[161] Acts 6:5.

[162] Acts 6:8.

[163] Acts 6:9–10.

These men stirred up the people, elders, and scribes. They came to Stephen and brought him to the council. They had false witnesses say, "*This man ceaseth not to speak blasphemous words against this holy place, and the law: For we have heard him say, that this Jesus of Nazareth shall destroy this place, and shall change the customs which Moses delivered us.*"

Those who sat in the council looked intently at Stephen. Though Stephen was brought into the council and falsely accused, his face was like that of an angel.[164] When the high priest asked Stephen if these things were true, he responded boldly.[165]

After hearing Stephen's message, they were cut to the heart. They gnashed at him with their teeth. But being full of the Holy Spirit, Stephen steadfastly looked into heaven, seeing the glory of God and Jesus standing at the right hand of God. Stephen said, "*Behold, I see the heavens opened, and the Son of man standing on the right hand of God.*"[166]

Those in the council cried with a loud voice. They closed their ears and rushed him. They cast Stephen out of the city and stoned him. The witnesses laid

---

[164] Acts 6:11–15.

[165] Luke 12:11–12; Acts 7:1–53.

[166] Acts 7:54–56.

their clothes at the feet of a Pharisee named Saul, who gave his approval to Stephen's stoning and death.[167]

As they stoned Stephen, he called upon God, "*Lord Jesus, receive my spirit.*"[168] Then he kneeled down and cried with a loud voice, "*Lay not this sin to their charge.*" After saying this, he died.[169]

Stephen was a man full of faith, the Holy Spirit, and power. The Spirit moved through him to accomplish great wonders and miracles among the people. In spite of the opposition, persecution, false accusations, and unjust stoning, the joy of heaven was seen on his face and in his words. Stephen's life stands as a testimony for the joy set before him.

---

[167] Acts 7:57–58, 8:1.

[168] Acts 7:59.

[169] Acts 7:59–60.

Expression of Joy

Saul ravaged the church. He entered into every house and hauled men and women to prison.[170] Besides the apostles, the church scattered abroad, preaching the word of God.[171]

Saul continued to threaten and slaughter the disciples of the Lord. He went to the high priest requesting permission to travel to the synagogues in Damascus. He wanted to search for men and women belonging to the church in order to bind and return them to Jerusalem.[172]

---

[170] Acts 8:3.

[171] Acts 8:4.

[172] Acts 9:1–2.

While on the way to Damascus, a light from heaven shined around Saul, and he fell to the ground. He heard a voice say to him, *"Saul, Saul, why persecutest thou me?"* Saul immediately recognized the Lord and asked who He was. The Lord said, *"I am Jesus whom thou persecutest: it is hard for thee to kick against the pricks."* Both shaking and astonished, Saul asked what the Lord wanted him to do. The Lord told him to go into Damascus, and he would be told what to do. The men who were with him were speechless. They heard a voice but did not see anyone. When Saul stood up and opened his eyes, he was blind. He had to be led by the hand into the city. Saul did not eat or drink for three days.[173]

The Lord then sent a man named Ananias to him to restore his sight and be filled with the Holy Ghost.[174] The Lord told Ananias that Saul was a chosen vessel unto Him.[175] He would bear the Lord's name before the Gentiles, kings, and the children of Israel. The Lord would show Saul what great things he must suffer for His name's sake.[176]

In the years that followed, Saul, who later used his Roman name Paul, served the Lord as an apostle of

---

[173] Acts 9:5–9.

[174] Acts 9:11–12, 17.

[175] Acts 9:15.

[176] Acts 9:16.

Jesus Christ. He went on three missionary journeys throughout Europe and Asia Minor. Through his journeys, Paul:

1. received thirty-nine lashes from the Jews on five separate occasions,[177]
2. was beaten with rods three times,
3. was stoned once,
4. was shipwrecked three times,
5. was adrift at sea for a day and a half,[178]
6. was exposed to dangers of rivers and robbers and dangers in the city, wilderness, on the seas, and among false brothers,[179]
7. was wearied and in pain,
8. was unable to sleep,
9. often went without food or water,
10. was at times cold and naked.[180]

Yet, in spite of what he suffered, Paul's commitment to Christ did not waver:

For which cause we faint not; but though our outward man perish, yet the inward man is renewed day by day. For our light affliction, which is but for a

---

[177] 2 Corinthians 11:24.

[178] 2 Corinthians 11:25.

[179] 2 Corinthians 11:26.

[180] 2 Corinthians 11:27.

moment, worketh for us a far more exceeding and eternal weight of glory; While we look not at the things which are seen, but at the things which are not seen: for the things which are seen are temporal; but the things which are not seen are eternal.

2 CORINTHIANS 4:16–18

On Paul's second missionary journey, he and Silas traveled to the city of Philippi. While there, a woman with a spirit of divination followed them. She shouted how they were men of the most high God, showing them the way of salvation.[181] After a few days of this, Paul became grieved. He turned to the spirit and commanded it come out of her, and it did.[182]

Her masters used her divination for profit, but now, her power was gone. The masters took Paul and Silas and brought them to the magistrates. They charged them with bringing trouble to the city.[183] Her masters said Paul and Silas, as Jews, were teaching customs that were not lawful for Romans to receive. After the multitude had rosed up against them, the magistrates commanded they be beaten with rods and cast into prison.[184]

---

[181] Acts 16:16–17.

[182] Acts 16:18.

[183] Acts 16:19–20.

[184] Acts 16:21–22.

Placed in the inner prison with their feet in the stocks, Paul and Silas were praying and singing praises to God at midnight.[185] They sang loud enough for the other prisoners to hear them. Suddenly, there was a great earthquake, and the prison foundations shook. Then all the prison doors opened, and everyone's bonds were loosed.[186]

The prison keeper who was commanded to guard Paul and Silas awoke from his sleep. Thinking the prisoners escaped when he saw the open prison doors, he pulled out his sword to kill himself. But Paul cried out saying, *"Do thyself no harm: for we are all here."*[187]

Recognizing the power of God, the prison keeper called for a light, went inside, and fell down before Paul and Silas trembling. After bringing them out, he asked them, *"What must I do to be saved?"*[188] They told him to believe on the Lord Jesus Christ, then he and everyone in his household will be saved. Paul and Silas then spoke to the prison keeper and everyone in his house about the word of the Lord.[189]

---

[185] Acts 16:25.

[186] Acts 16:26.

[187] Acts 16:27–28.

[188] Acts 16:29–30.

[189] Acts 16:31–32.

And at that same hour of the night, the prison keeper cleaned their wounds and he and his household were baptized.[190] The prison keeper brought Paul and Silas into his house and prepared a meal for them. He and his household rejoiced, believing in God.[191]

We are troubled on every side, yet not distressed; we are perplexed, but not in despair; Persecuted, but not forsaken; cast down, but not destroyed; Always bearing about in the body the dying of the Lord Jesus, that the life also of Jesus might be made manifest in our body. For we which live are always delivered unto death for Jesus' sake, that the life also of Jesus might be made manifest in our mortal flesh.

2 CORINTHIANS 4:8–11

Through Paul and Silas, the life of Jesus was made manifest because they remained joyful in spite of their circumstances. God used their situation to bring glory to Himself and add to the family of God—*at midnight.*

---

[190] Acts 16:33.

[191] Acts 16:34.

A Life of Joy

While in a Roman prison, Paul wrote a letter to the church in Philippi. He thanked them for sending Epaphroditus, along with their gift of provisions.[192] Paul shared his secret of being content in any situation and spoke about his status in prison.[193] He also shared several recurring themes of joy, rejoicing, and being like-minded.

Requests with joy—Philippians 1:1–7

In opening his letter, Paul expresses his thankfulness to God every time He remembers them. And in every prayer for them, he makes his requests

---

[192] Philippians 2:25–30.

[193] Philippians 1:12–15.

with joy. Paul considers his fellowship with them in the gospel from the very first day. He knows God has begun a good work in them and will perform it until the day of Jesus Christ. Paul feels it is right for him to think this way about them because they are in his heart. Through both his chains and in the defense and confirmation of the gospel, they are partakers of his grace.

Philippians 1:8–14—God is his witness for how he longs after them in the affections of Jesus Christ. He prays that their love will abound more and more in knowledge and all discernment. This will allow them to discern things that are excellent and be sincere and without offense until the day of Christ. On this day, they will be filled with the fruits of righteousness given by Jesus Christ, to the glory and praise of God.

Paul wanted the Philippians to know what has happened to him is causing the spread of the gospel. Everyone in the palace and all other places know about his bonds in Christ. And through his bonds, many brothers in the Lord are speaking the word more boldly without fear.

Rejoice in the preaching of Christ— Philippians 1:15–18

Among those preaching Christ, Paul learned there were two groups. One group was not sincere in their preaching. They were preaching out of jealousy and contention. The other group was preaching out of love, knowing Paul was set for the defense of the gospel. He rejoices because whether either group is preaching in pretense or truth, Christ is being preached.

Joy in the faith—Philippians 1:19–26

Through the Philippians' prayer and supply of the Spirit of Jesus Christ, Paul knows that these situations will turn out to his salvation. He will not be ashamed in any way according to his earnest expectation and hope. Whether through death or life and with all boldness, Christ will be magnified in his body. For Paul, to live is Christ and to die is gain. If Paul continues living, he will be fruitful in his labor, but he is not sure which he should choose. He has a desire to depart and be with Christ, which is far better. But it will be more necessary for them if he lives. With this confidence, Paul knows that he will remain with them. He will continue with them for their progress and joy in the faith so that their rejoicing might be more abundant in Jesus Christ upon his return to them again.

Philippians 1:27–30—Paul reminds them to only allow their lives to be worthy of the gospel of Christ. So whether he comes and sees them again or remains absent, he wants them to stand fast in one spirit, strive together with one mind for the faith of the gospel, and not be afraid of their adversaries. Their fearlessness will be the evidence of their adversaries' pending destruction, but for them, it is a sign of their salvation and that of God. On behalf of Christ, they have been given the opportunity to not only believe in Him but also to suffer on His behalf; having the same conflicts that they saw Paul had and hear about now.

Having complete joy—Philippians 2:1–8

Paul continues his message by saying if there is any consolation in Christ, comfort of love, fellowship of the Spirit, and affection and compassion, to make his joy complete by being like-minded, having the same love toward one another, being of one accord, of one mind. Paul provides further instructions on how they should conduct themselves before telling them the type of mind they all should have (and share together)—the same mind that was in Christ Jesus who:

1. made Himself of no reputation,
2. took the form of a servant,
3. humbled Himself,
4. became obedient unto death.

Who, being in the form of God, thought it not robbery to be equal with God: But made himself of no reputation, and took upon him the form of a servant,

*and was made in the likeness of men: And being
found in fashion as a man, he humbled himself, and
became obedient unto death, even the death of the
cross. Wherefore God also hath highly exalted him,
and given him a name which is above every name:
That at the name of Jesus every knee should bow, of
things in heaven, and things in earth, and things
under the earth; And that every tongue should confess
that Jesus Christ is Lord, to the glory of God the
Father.*

PHILIPPIANS 2:6–11

Rejoicing together—Philippians 2:12–18

As the Philippians have always obeyed the Lord in
both Paul's presence and even more in his absence, he
told them to work out their salvation with fear and
trembling. It is God working in them to both will and
work for His good pleasure. In this, Paul tells them to
do all things without murmuring or disputing. This
will allow them to become blameless and harmless,
children of God without defect in the midst of a
crooked and perverse generation. They will be seen as
lights in the world, holding up the word of life.

Paul will then boast in the day of Christ, seeing
that he did not run or labor among them in vain.
Even if his life is lost on the sacrifice and service of
their faith, he will rejoice, and rejoice with them. Paul
wants them to rejoice, and rejoice with him.

Philippians 2:19–30—Paul is trusting in the Lord to be able to send Timothy to them shortly. He will be comforted in knowing how they are doing. Paul says he has no one as likeminded as Timothy, who genuinely cares for their state. Though many seek to advance their own interests and not the things of Jesus Christ, Paul said they know of Timothy's character; how he serves with Paul in the gospel as a son with his father. He hopes to send Timothy as soon as he finds out how things will go with him. But Paul also hopes to come himself shortly.

Rejoice in the saints—Philippians 2:25–30

Paul believes it is necessary to send Epaphroditus back to Philippi. Paul considers him as his brother, companion in labor, and fellow soldier. Epaphroditus was troubled and longed after the Philippians when they heard he was sick. Paul confirms Epaphroditus was sick and close to death, but God showed him mercy. He says God also showed him mercy in the matter, for fear that he would have had sorrow upon sorrow. As such, Paul is sending Epaphroditus back to Philippi, so when they see him again, they can rejoice, and he can be less sorrowful. Paul asks them to receive Epaphroditus in the Lord with all gladness. He also asks them to hold others like Epaphroditus in such honor as he was close to death because of the work of Christ. Epaphroditus did not regard his own life to provide what was lacking in their service toward him.

Rejoice in the Lord—Philippians 3:1–3

Paul tells the Philippians to rejoice in the Lord. Though he told them this before, he does not feel it is tiresome for him to repeat but safe for them. He says to beware of the dogs, evils workers, and those who mutilate the flesh. The comparison Paul provides is that of a true and false circumcision. He says they are of the circumcision who worship God in the Spirit, rejoice in Christ Jesus, and have no confidence in the flesh.

Philippians 3:4–21—Paul could also have confidence in the flesh, and even more if anyone else thinks they have any trust in the flesh. His confidence would come from his position as a Hebrew:

1. circumcised on the eighth day,
2. of the nation of Israel from the tribe of Benjamin,
3. a Hebrew of Hebrews,
4. as to the law (of Moses), a Pharisee,
5. concerning his zeal, he persecuted the church,
6. concerning righteousness that is found in (observing) the law, he was blameless.

But in all these things that were once a benefit for Paul, he counts as a loss for Christ. He counts all things to be a loss for the excellency of the knowledge of Christ Jesus his Lord, for whom he suffered the loss of all things. He counts them as refuse so that he might win Christ. Paul wants to be found in Christ, not having his own righteousness from the law, but through the faith of Christ, the righteousness that is of God by faith. This allows Paul to know Him, the power of His resurrection, and the fellowship of His sufferings, where he is conformed unto His death—this is, if by any means—he can attain to the resurrection of the dead.

Paul is not saying that he has already obtained it or has been made perfect, but he presses on so he can obtain what he was taken hold of by Christ Jesus. Paul does not consider that he has taken hold of it, but what he does is forget those things which are behind him and stretch forward to those things that are before him. He presses toward the mark for the high calling of God in Christ Jesus.

Paul wants as many of them that are perfect to think this way. If anyone thinks differently, he knows God will also reveal this to them. But to the extent they have already attained, Paul says, '*let us*' walk by the same rule and sentiment. As the Philippians have Paul (and others) as an example, he wants them to be followers of his example and take heed to those who walk as such. But many walk—as Paul told them often, and even weeping now—as enemies of the cross. Their end is destruction, their god is their belly, their glory is their shame, and they mind earthly things. But their citizenship is in heaven, from where they also look for the Savior, the Lord Jesus Christ. He will change their vile bodies so they might be made like His glorious body—by the power that allows Him to subject all things to Himself.

Paul's joy and crown—Philippians 4:1–3

As Paul prepares to conclude his letter, he provides several messages of encouragement and instruction. He calls them his dearly beloved brethren that he longs for—his joy and crown.

Rejoice in the Lord always—Philippians 4:4

Again, Paul tells them to rejoice in the Lord always, and again he says, *rejoice*.

Philippians 4:5–9—As the Lord is at hand, they should let their gentleness be known to all men. They should not be anxious about anything, but in everything, they should present their requests to God through prayer and petition with thanksgiving. When they do this, the peace of God—which surpasses all understanding—will guard their hearts and minds through Christ Jesus.

Paul explains they should think about things that are:

1. true,
2. honorable,

3. just,
4. pure,
5. lovely,
6. of good report,
7. of any virtue,
8. of any praise.

Paul goes on to say that if they do those things they have learned, received, heard, and saw in him, the God of peace will be with them.

Rejoice in caring—Philippians 4:10–13

Paul rejoiced in the Lord when they renewed their concern for him. It was not that they were not concerned before, but they had no opportunity to show it. Paul was not making this statement because he had a particular need, as he has learned how to be content in whatever situation he might find himself. He learned the secret of facing both abundance and lack, for he can do all things through Christ who strengthens him.

Philippians 4:14–23—Paul acknowledges how they did well in sharing with his affliction. After his first visit of sharing the gospel and leaving from Macedonia, no other church besides theirs communicated with him concerning giving and receiving. Even when he was in Thessalonica, they supplied for his needs more than once. This was not because Paul sought for a gift, but he desires fruit that might increase their account. But Paul says he has all he needs and more. He is full after receiving the things they sent to him by Epaphroditus: a sweet-smelling fragrance, a sacrifice acceptable and well-pleasing to God. Paul says God will supply their every need according to His riches in glory by Christ Jesus. Paul closes his instructions and encouragements:

Now unto God and our Father be the glory forever and ever. Amen.

Lastly, Paul concludes his letter with salutations:

1. salute every saint in Christ Jesus,
2. the brethren with him greet them,
3. all the saints salute them, namely those of Caesar's household.

The grace of our Lord Jesus Christ be with you all. Amen.

Overcome with Joy

About sixty-five years after Jesus' death and ascension, John was exiled to the island of Patmos for preaching the word of God and the testimony of Jesus Christ.[194] While on the island, God gave him the Revelation of Jesus Christ. The word of this prophecy was written to the seven churches in Asia.[195] He wanted John to write what he sees—both the things that are happening now and things that will happen later.[196]

As He began to share His revelation, Jesus sent messages to each of the seven churches. One church was enduring patiently, and another was about to face

---

[194] Revelation 1:9.

[195] Revelation 1:1–3.

[196] Revelation 1:1, 19–20.

a short season of suffering. The others required correction. But each church received a promise for overcoming. These promises were not only for the seven churches. *Anyone* who has an ear to hear can receive the same promises. Much, if not all, of what Jesus spoke to each church is occurring in our churches today. Take heed. Pray. Remain watchful.

Ephesus—Revelation 2:1–7

The one who holds the seven stars in His right hand and walks in the midst of the seven golden candlesticks knew their works, labors, and patience. He knew they could not bear those who were evil. They examined those who said they were apostles and discovered those who were lying. They persevered and endured for His name's sake and have not grown weary. They have also hated the deeds of the Nicolaitanes, which Jesus also hates. But there was something He *somewhat* had against them.

Though the church in Ephesus stood for their faith, the church left their first love. He told them to remember from where they fell, repent, and do the first works. If they do not repent, Jesus will come to them quickly and remove their candlestick (church) from its place.

To him that overcometh will I give to eat of the tree of life, which is in the midst of the paradise of God.

Smyrna—Revelation 2:8–11

The first and the last, which was dead and is now alive said He knew their works, tribulation, and poverty (though they are rich). He knew the blasphemy of those posing as Jews but are of the synagogue of Satan.

Jesus told them not to fear the things they were about to suffer. The devil will cast some of them into prison—that they might be tried and examined—facing tribulation for ten days. If they are faithful, even unto death, He will give them a crown of life.

He that overcometh shall not be hurt of the second death.

Pergamum—Revelation 2:12–17

He who has the sharp sword with two edges said He knew their works and where they dwell, and even where Satan's throne is. They had held fast to Jesus' name and have not denied His faith, even when Antipas, His faithful martyr, was killed among them, where Satan dwells. But Jesus had a few things against them.

Some in the church have held to the doctrine of Balaam, who placed a stumbling block before the children of Israel, to eat things sacrificed to idols and commit fornication.[197] They also had some who held

---

[197] Numbers 31:1–20.

to the doctrine of the Nicolaitanes, which is something Jesus hates. He said if they did not repent, He would come to them quickly and fight against them with the sword of His mouth.

To him that overcometh will I give to eat of the hidden manna, and will give him a white stone, and in the stone a new name written, which no man knoweth saving he that receiveth it.

Thyatira—Revelation 2:18–29

The Son of God, who has eyes like a flame of fire and feet like brass said He knew their works, charity, service, faith, and patience. Their latest works exceed their first. But Jesus had a few things against them.

The church allowed Jezebel—who calls herself a prophetess—to teach and seduce His servants to commit fornication and eat things sacrificed to idols. Jesus gave her time to repent, but she did not. And unless she and those who commit adultery with her repent, He will cast them into a bed of great tribulation. Jesus will kill her children, and all the churches will know that He searches the minds and hearts and gives to everyone according to their deeds.

But to the rest that does not follow the doctrine (from Jezebel) and does not know the deep mysteries of Satan, Jesus says He will place no other burden upon them. They should hold fast to what they have already until He comes.

And he that overcometh, and keepeth my works unto the end, to him will I give power over the nations: And he shall rule them with a rod of iron; as the vessels of a potter shall they be broken to shivers: even as I received of my Father. And I will give him the morning star.

Sardis—Revelation 3:1–6

He who has the seven Spirits of God and the seven stars said He knew their works—how they have a reputation of being alive—but are dead. He told them to be watchful and strengthen what remains—those things ready to die—because He has not found their works perfect unto God. Jesus told them to remember how they received and heard, to hold fast, and repent. If they do not keep watch, He will come upon them as a thief, for they will not know what hour He will come to them.

Jesus mentioned that there are a few people in Sardis who have not defiled their garments. They will walk with Him in white because they are worthy.

He that overcometh, the same shall be clothed in white raiment; and I will not blot out his name out of the book of life, but I will confess his name before my Father, and before his angels.

Philadelphia—Revelation 3:7–13

He who is holy, true, and has the key of David—who opens and no man shuts, and shuts and no man opens—said He knew their works.[198] He set before them an open door, and no man can shut it because they have kept His word and have not denied His name, even though they have a little strength.

Jesus spoke about those among them who say they are Jews but are not. They lie because they are of the synagogue of Satan. He will make them come to the Philadelphians and worship before their feet and to know that He has loved them.

Because they have kept the word of His patience, Jesus will keep them from the hour of temptation that will come upon the world. This temptation will try those who dwell upon the earth. He told them that He was coming quickly and to hold fast to what they have so that no man takes their crown.

Him that overcometh will I make a pillar in the temple of my God, and he shall go no more out: and I will write upon him the name of my God, and the name of the city of my God, which is new Jerusalem, which cometh down out of heaven from my God: and I will write upon him my new name.

---

[198] Isaiah 22:22; 1 John 5:20; Revelation 3:7.

Laodicea—Revelation 3:14–22

The Amen, the faithful and true witness, the beginning of the creation of God said He knew their works.[199] They are neither cold nor hot—and He wished they were cold or hot. But because they are lukewarm and neither cold nor hot, Jesus will spew them out of His mouth.

The Laodiceans said they were rich, increased with goods, and did not need anything. But they did not realize they were wretched, miserable, poor, blind, and naked. Jesus told them to buy gold from Him tried in the fire so they might be rich, clothe themselves with white clothing so the shame of their nakedness is not seen, and anoint their eyes with eye salve so they might see.

Jesus said that as many as He loves, He rebukes and disciplines.[200] He wants them to be zealous and repent. Jesus stands at the door and knocks. If anyone hears His voice and opens the door, He will eat with him, and he with Jesus.

To him that overcometh will I grant to sit with me in my throne, even as I also overcame, and am set down with my Father in his throne.

---

[199] Colossians 1:15–19.

[200] Hebrews 12:9–13.

As many as Jesus loves, He rebukes and disciplines. Jesus loved the men and women in the seven churches. Though a church lost their love for Him, was lukewarm, engaged in fornication, and was dead, He was calling them to repent and turn back to Him. Jesus even gave Jezebel two separate occasions to repent of her conduct.

God did not give up on the seven churches, and He has not given up on you. He showers you with His grace and disciplines you because He loves you. He is providing you an opportunity to live for Him— to love Him with all your heart, soul, and mind, experience His joy, and be with Him forever.[201]

Behold, the tabernacle of God is with men, and he will dwell with them, and they shall be his people, and God himself shall be with them, and be their God. And God shall wipe away all tears from their eyes; and there shall be no more death, neither sorrow, nor crying, neither shall there be any more pain: for the former things are passed away. And he that sat upon the throne said, Behold, I make all things new. And he said unto me, Write: for these words are true and faithful. And he said unto me, It is done. I am Alpha and Omega, the beginning and the end. I will give unto him that is athirst of the fountain of the water of life freely. He that overcometh shall inherit

---

[201] Matthew 22:36–40; Romans 6:1–11.

all things; and I will be his God, and he shall be my son.

REVELATION 21:3–7

Stand for Joy

Finally, my brethren, be strong in the Lord, and in the power of his might. Put on the whole armour of God, that ye may be able to stand against the wiles of the devil. For we wrestle not against flesh and blood, but against principalities, against powers, against the rulers of the darkness of this world, against spiritual wickedness in high places. Wherefore take unto you the whole armour of God, that ye may be able to withstand in the evil day, and having done all, to stand. Stand therefore, having your loins girt about with truth, and having on the breastplate of righteousness; And your feet shod with the preparation of the gospel of peace; Above all, taking the shield of faith, wherewith ye shall be able to quench all the fiery darts of the wicked. And take the helmet of salvation, and the sword of the Spirit, which is the word of God: Praying always with all prayer and supplication in the

Spirit, and watching thereunto with all perseverance and supplication for all saints

EPHESIANS 6:10–18

Your fleshly lusts and Satan do not want you to experience the joy you have read about in this book. They want you to be consumed and distracted with people, places, and things—remaining self-centered, miserable, angry, unforgiving, and disobedient—everything a life in Christ is not. Even the slightest stain of sin can affect your life in God. So you must stand. Stand through:

1. pain,
2. suffering,
3. silence,
4. tragedy,
5. temptation,
6. mental and physical attacks.

Thank God you can do all things through Christ who strengthens you. God can sustain you and bear your burdens.[202] *You can stand in Him!*

Praise God that you can come to Him at any time in prayer.[203] You can saturate your heart, soul, and mind with His word. You can seek Him through your

---

[202] Psalm 55:22; Matthew 11:28–30; 1 Peter 5:6–7.

[203] Psalm 55:17; Isaiah 1:18.

praise and worship. You can be encouraged and sharpened through your fellowship.[204]

I am a living witness of His ability to help you sort out and press through the pain and darkness in your heart, soul, and mind to find joy in Him. There are days when I have to continually stay before God in prayer, His word, and listen to uplifting gospel music. In these moments, it feels like Satan and my flesh are trying to overwhelm me with despair, sadness, and temptation, but I run to the Lord. He is my strong tower.[205] He will raise up a standard against the enemy.[206] He strengthens me to continue standing.

I cannot give Satan or my flesh any room to operate in my life.[207] I must remain watchful and sober because the enemy is roaming, waiting for his moment to strike.[208] I must place my complete trust in the Lord because I will not make it without Him...

Trust in the Lord with all thine heart; and lean not unto thine own understanding. In all thy ways acknowledge him, and he shall direct thy paths.

PROVERBS 3:5–6

---

[204] Proverbs 27:17; Galatians 6:1–2.

[205] Psalm 18:2, 61:1–3; Proverbs 18:10.

[206] Isaiah 59:19.

[207] Ephesians 4:27; 2 Timothy 2:22; James 4:7.

[208] 1 Peter 5:8–9.

Trusting in the Lord with all my heart means I cannot place any confidence in my own thoughts or prior ways of thinking. In all my ways and in everything I do, I must acknowledge His will, His way, and His purpose. I must acknowledge His sovereignty over my life and live as He desires: where, when, and how. Only then can the Lord direct my paths. See, if I am trusting in myself, trying to do things my way, or I am unwilling to relinquish my life over to Him, I will not follow Him. I will not listen. I will go my own way, experiencing deep sadness, pain, and sin—far from the joy God wants me to experience in Him. So I must choose to stand in spite of what is occurring around me (and sometimes within me)...*I must stand.*

Conclusion

As *Joy: The Eternal Gift of God* concludes, I pray you have gained an expanded view of what it means to have and experience joy. Yes, joy is gladness, calm delight, and rejoicing. But most of all, experiencing joy is having God—loving Him with all your heart, soul, and mind and awaiting the promise of eternal life in His presence. To experience this joy, you must live a consecrated life through your love for Him and obedience to His word and will.[209] Your obedience to His commands will reflect His glory and His purpose to make His love and salvation known to the world. This is the same love that drew you to Him, and it is the same love He desires you to display to others.

I pray you will be faithful in following Jesus' commands and the life and purpose He has given you to fulfill. God has not given you anything you cannot

---

[209] 1 John 5:2–6.

handle.[210]   Whatever He is calling you to do, be faithful and do it with joy. Serve the Lord. Do not lose heart. Be strong. Keep your trust in Him. An eternal reward of joy awaits you.[211]

But ye, beloved, building up yourselves on your most holy faith, praying in the Holy Ghost, Keep yourselves in the love of God, looking for the mercy of our Lord Jesus Christ unto eternal life. And of some have compassion, making a difference: And others save with fear, pulling them out of the fire; hating even the garment spotted by the flesh. Now unto him that is able to keep you from falling, and to present you faultless before the presence of his glory with exceeding joy, To the only wise God our Saviour, be glory and majesty, dominion and power, both now and ever. Amen.

JUDE 20–25

---

[210] 1 Corinthians 10:12–14.

[211] Hebrews 11:6.

(com)mission
PUBLISHING

www.commissionpubs.com
info@commissionpubs.com